GRATITUDE

EMBRACING THANKFULNESS FOR A LIFE OF PURPOSE, AUTHENTICITY, AND FULFILLMENT

Book 2 in the Life Source Series

GRATITUDE

EMBRACING THANKFULNESS FOR A LIFE OF PURPOSE, AUTHENTICITY, AND FULFILLMENT

JEFF HUSTON & GABE OLSON

ethos
collective

Published by Igniting Souls
PO Box 43, Powell, OH 43065
IgnitingSouls.com

LCCN: 2025913401
Paperback ISBN: 978-1-63680-543-6
Hardcover ISBN: 978-1-63680-544-3
e-Book ISBN: 978-1-63680-545-0

Available in paperback, hardcover, e-book, and audiobook.

And we know that in all things God works for the good of those who love him, who have been called according to his purpose.
—Romans 8:28

TABLE OF CONTENTS

CHAPTER 1

ASSESSING YOUR GRATITUDE

In today's world, it's easy to feel like we are always missing out on something. With so many people around us achieving great things and having exciting experiences, it's hard not to compare our lives to theirs. But what if the key to happiness isn't having more but appreciating what we already have?

In our book, *Life Source,* we shared . . .

We're beginning this journey with a posture that's simple in theory, but deeply powerful in practice: gratitude. And not just the surface-level kind that flickers when everything goes our way, but a rooted, steady sort of gratitude. The kind that holds us together in the middle of the mess. It's no accident that gratitude is the starting point in our GRACIE journey—it's the ground we build everything else on.

Let's face it: the world doesn't nudge us toward gratitude. It pulls us in the opposite direction—toward striving, comparing, accumulating. There's always something newer, better, shinier. If we're not careful, we can get swept up in the chase and lose sight of the good that's already right in front of us.

But something shifts when we start from gratitude. When we wake up and decide to name what's good before we start listing what's lacking, suddenly, we see with clearer eyes. We begin to realize that even in the mundane, even in the mess, there's something worth celebrating. Gratitude slows us down long enough to notice.

Self-Assessment for Gratitude

Self-assessment is an influential tool that helps us understand our thoughts, feelings, and behaviors. When it comes to cultivating gratitude, a focused mindset combined with an honest self-assessment can be incredibly valuable. These allow us to reflect on our experiences, recognize the positive aspects of our lives, and make conscious choices to be grateful. By looking inward and evaluating our mindset, we can develop a deeper sense of appreciation for what we have, even during difficult times.

Imagine you've had a particularly tough week at work. Deadlines were tight, projects were challenging, and you felt overwhelmed. At the end of the week, you decide to do an honest self-assessment to understand your thoughts and feelings and see how they impacted your week overall.

You sit down with a journal, start reflecting on your experiences, and write about the stressful moments and how they made you feel. But then, you shift your focus to look for positive aspects. You realize that despite the challenges, you completed all your tasks, and you recall a moment when a colleague praised your work, which made you feel appreciated. You remember how your family supported you by giving you space to work and caring for household chores.

Through this honest self-assessment, you recognize that while the week was tough, it also had positive elements. You start to appreciate your resilience, the support from your family, and the acknowledgment from your colleagues. This reflection helps you feel more grateful for the good things in your life, even in the midst of difficulties.

Regularly practicing this kind of honest self-assessment can train your mind to notice and appreciate positive aspects more readily, enhancing your overall sense of gratitude.

The Gap and The Gain®

Dan Sullivan, co-founder of Strategic Coach®, created the concept of The Gap and The Gain and believes it is an essential aspect of personal growth. The "gap" represents the difference between where we currently are and our desired goals in various life areas, such as careers, relationships, or skills. Recognizing these gaps is crucial for providing clarity and direction in our growth journey. Conversely, "gain" signifies the progress made towards closing the gap and achieving our objectives. Celebrating our gains, regardless of size, keeps us motivated in our pursuit of personal development.

Taking time to assess ourselves means embracing the gain, not the gap. Dan Sullivan and Dr. Benjamin Hardy introduced this concept in their book, *The Gap and The*

Gain: The High Achievers' Guide to Happiness, Confidence, and Success.[1] Rather than fixating on unattainable goals—the horizon or gap—the focus shifts to appreciating how far we've come—the gain. This perspective shift fosters positivity and spurs motivation.

For instance, when learning to play the piano, initially aiming to master a challenging piece may seem daunting, creating a gap between the current skill level and the goal. However, reflecting on progress reveals significant gain—the ability to play simpler songs and improved skills. Focusing on this progress motivates continued practice. Recognizing gain is vital as success markers continually shift, perpetuating the gap. Thus, maintaining a positive mindset through gratitude becomes essential.

Self-assessment prompts goal setting for gratitude and encourages daily acknowledgment of something to be thankful for. Actively seeking and recognizing positives fosters a gain-focused mindset, improving overall mood and outlook.

Keeping A Gratitude Journal

A gratitude journal can help create a mindset grounded in gratitude. It can be as simple as a notebook to record things you're thankful for each day.

Journaling is an effective way to use honest self-assessment. By writing down the things we are thankful for each day, we create a record of what we're grateful for, reinforcing a

---

[1]   Dan Sullivan and Benjamin Hardy, *The Gap and the Gain: The High Achievers Guide to Happiness, Confidence, and Success* (Carlsbad, CA: Hay House, Inc, 2021).

grateful mindset. Keeping a gratitude journal is like creating a special book where we write down things we're thankful for every day. It's a way to record all the blessings we experience. This helps us focus on the positive and can make us feel happier overall. Over time, as we continue this habit, it becomes easier to see the good in each day, even when life becomes overwhelming

Here are some ideas for maintaining a journal:

- *Set a consistent time.* Choose morning or evening, and create a rhythm that becomes part of your day.

- *Use simple prompts.* Ask yourself: What made me smile today? What gave me peace? Who showed me love?

- *Be as specific as possible.* Instead of "I'm thankful for my job," try "I'm thankful I got to solve a tough problem today and felt capable."

- *Celebrate the little stuff.* The big moments are great—but it's the small, ordinary ones that create a life of gratitude.

- *Review often.* Look back through your entries once a week or once a month. Let them remind you how much goodness is woven into your life.

The key is to find a method that feels meaningful and enjoyable to you, so journaling will become a regular part of your routine.

Essentially, honest self-assessment helps us regularly check in with ourselves, recognize the good, and consciously choose to be grateful. This can lead to a happier, more content life—even in the face of challenges. By reflecting on our experiences and focusing on what we have, we can cultivate a deeper sense of gratitude—a mindset of appreciation.

Choosing Gratitude in Trials

Choosing gratitude amidst trials is important because it helps shift our focus from what's going wrong to what's still good in our lives. When we face challenges, it's easy to get overwhelmed by negativity and despair. However, by actively choosing to find things to be grateful for, we can maintain a more positive outlook, reduce stress, and build resilience. Gratitude reminds us of the blessings we still have, even during difficult times, and it can help us find hope and strength to overcome obstacles. Ultimately, practicing gratitude amidst trials can lead to greater emotional well-being and a more optimistic perspective on life.

Jesus shows us how to choose gratitude even during tough times. He faced great suffering but stayed connected to God's will and found reasons to be grateful. This teaches us that gratitude isn't about being thankful for the hardships themselves but for the growth and deeper understanding that come from the experience of hardship. We can follow Jesus's example in our lives by choosing how to respond in gratitude.

When the situation is challenging, and it's hard to see the positive aspects, this powerful mindset reminds us of John 16:13: "In this world, you will have trouble. But take heart! I have overcome the world." Yes, He overcame the world, yes, He defeated death, and yes, He made a way against impossible odds for us to spend eternity with Him! In the hardest moments of life, that truth remains for Christians. I'm not sure where you, as a reader, are, but I would encourage you to take an assessment of your life. Do you have that hope?

Being Grateful in Experiences

There's an important distinction between being grateful *for* an experience and being grateful *in* it. Both matter, but one is easier than the other.

Being grateful *for* something usually comes after the fact. You look back on a promotion, a gift, a good day—and you're thankful. And that's good.

But being grateful *in* something? That's different.

That's looking around in real time and choosing to find goodness before the outcome is clear. It's finding purpose while you're still in the middle of the waiting. It's learning to say, "Even here, there's something good."

When we train ourselves to live this way, we become more present. We stop rushing past the moment in search of the next. Gratitude anchors us to the now, and in that space, we grow.

Go B.I.G.—Begin In Gratitude

In a world often filled with challenges, "Go B.I.G.—Begin In Gratitude" reminds us to start each day with appreciation. It means focusing on the positives from the get-go, no matter how tough things seem. By taking a moment each morning to reflect on what we're thankful for, we set a positive tone for the day ahead. Beginning with gratitude helps shift our mindsets from what we lack to what we have, fostering positivity and abundance. It also sets a firm intention for the day, attracting healthier thoughts into our lives. When we start with gratitude, we're better equipped to navigate challenges and find solutions with adaptability. Ultimately, "Go B.I.G.—Begin In Gratitude" encourages us to cultivate a mindset of appreciation, empowering us to live each day with grace. That's why this book, the beginning of the GRACIE framework, focuses on gratitude.

The selection of "GRACIE" as the framework's namesake was not random but rooted in recognizing gratitude's transformative power. As the first letter of the framework, "G" serves as a beacon of hope and renewal, inviting individuals to explore self-discovery and personal empowerment.

Go B.I.G. reflects the heart of GRACIE's framework. It emphasizes starting each day with a grateful mindset, which can have remarkable, positive effects over time. Imagine waking up each morning and taking a moment to appreciate the simple things around you: the warmth of sunlight streaming through your window, the smell of freshly brewed coffee, or simply the ability to take another breath of fresh air. Acknowledging these small blessings sets a positive tone for the day ahead.

Throughout the day, you encounter various challenges, like getting stuck in traffic or facing a difficult task at work. Instead of dwelling on the negatives, gratitude chooses to approach these situations from a different vantage point.. Perhaps you're grateful for the opportunity to listen to your favorite music during the commute or for the chance to learn and grow from tackling a tough project. By consistently practicing gratitude in your daily life, you gradually shift your perspective and develop resilience in the face of adversity. You begin to see setbacks as opportunities for growth and as stepping stones toward your goals. This mindset shift not only enhances your overall well-being but also enriches your relationships and interactions with others, as you radiate positivity and appreciation in everything you do.

Biblical Transformative Power

And we know that in all things God works for the good of those who love him, who have been called according to his purpose.
—Romans 8:28

This Bible verse is like a comforting promise from God. It tells us that no matter what happens in our lives, whether it's something we like or something we don't, God can turn it into something good. It's like saying that even when bad things happen, God is still working behind the scenes to use what has happened for good and His glory. It's a reminder that God cares enough about each of us that no matter what has happened, good or bad, He can redeem it. In other words, He can use what everyone else thinks is bad and horrible and turn it into something beneficial and amazing.

Gratitude has a significant impact on our lives. It's like a magic power that can change the way we see things and how we feel. When we're thankful, it's like we put on special glasses that help us see all the good in stuff around us. We start noticing even the small blessings, like a friendly smile or a kind word, and we feel extraordinarily thankful for them. Gratitude doesn't just make us happy for a short time; it changes how we see the world around us. Instead of constantly thinking about what we don't have, we learn to appreciate what we do have. We feel a deep sense of calm and contentment that lasts. Being grateful isn't just about saying "thank you" for the good things; it's about making gratitude a part of how we live our lives every day.

When we realize how powerful gratitude is, we see the ways it can improve our lives. Gratitude becomes a key that opens the door to a happier and more contented life. It's like finding a hidden treasure—a source of joy and happiness that we didn't know was there. As we practice being grateful, we start to see all the good things in life, no matter how small they might seem. This new way of looking at things helps us deal with life's challenges in a better way. We become stronger and more resilient, knowing that even when things are tough, there are still things to be thankful for. By making gratitude a part of our daily lives, we embark on a journey toward a life filled with more peace, happiness, contentment, and joy.

Gratitude Assessment

Gratitude assessment means evaluating our level of appreciation. It involves asking yourself questions to determine growth or areas for growth. As you finish your day, rate yourself on a scale of one to ten, with one being rarely and ten indicating always.

- How many moments of my day did I view from the perspective of gratitude?

- How often did my mind default to the positive aspect of the event rather than the negative?
- How often did I recognize today's smallest blessings?

Assessing our level of gratitude allows us to become more aware of the positive aspects of our lives and appreciate them more fully. It also helps us understand the importance of gratitude in our overall well-being and encourages us to cultivate a thankful mindset.

For example, imagine you had a busy day at work. On your way home, you decide to do a quick gratitude assessment. Go back through your day and consider each event. Ask those three questions about each event. The answers will give you another opportunity to be thankful for the positive moments of your day, as well as see places that you might need to look at through a different lens.

By doing this regularly, you train your mind to focus on the positive, which can help you handle stress and challenges better.

Gratitude Reminders

To help remind yourself to be grateful, you could carry a gratitude chip in your pocket. This could be any small token that will remind you to say thank you throughout the day. Every time you touch it, say thank you for something around you.

A sticky note on your bathroom mirror can remind you to be grateful every morning, and a Bible verse on a note card to keep in your purse or your wallet can nudge you to be thankful each time you see it.

For example, a great Bible quote to focus on daily is, "So don't worry about tomorrow, for tomorrow will bring its own worries. Today's trouble is enough for today" (Matthew 6:34).

Just pick an action and get started. These small reminders can help you stay focused on being grateful in the present.

Self-assessment is for building gratitude. When we think about what we've been through, set goals to be thankful, write in a gratitude journal, and learn from Jesus's example, we appreciate life more and handle tough times better. Being grateful daily makes us feel more peaceful, content, happy, and joyful.

Therefore, do not worry about tomorrow,
for tomorrow will worry about itself.
—Matthew 6:34

CHAPTER 2

THE "15-MINUTE SYNDROME"

"I lived my life 15 minutes ahead. If I could do it all over again, I'd be more present in the moment." That statement launched a conversation about twenty years ago on a commercial flight. Usually, I keep to myself when flying, but something on that day compelled me to engage with the person in the next seat. I managed to get a free upgrade to first class due to my frequent flyer status and ended up next to an older gentleman, whom I presumed to be in his eighties, someone who had purchased his ticket. We engaged in small talk, and he mentioned he was a Veteran and it was his ninety-second birthday. He looked remarkably young for his age. Curious, I asked him for his best life advice. He responded, "I lived my life 15 minutes ahead." He explained how he constantly thought about future tasks, but looking back, he wished he had focused more on the present moment.

The "15-Minute Syndrome" is a term that describes focusing on what's coming up next instead of being present in the moment. Instead of enjoying what we're doing right now, our minds jump ahead to what we have to do next or what might happen soon. Whether it's thinking about the next task on our to-do list, worrying about an upcoming event, or anticipating a problem, this constant forward-thinking can leave us feeling hurried and stressed, as we're not fully experiencing or appreciating the present moment.

There's a good reason my friend on the plane experienced regret. The "15-Minute Syndrome" significantly impacts our ability to experience gratitude. First, it diminishes our enjoyment of the present moment. Preoccupation with what's coming doesn't allow us to fully engage and appreciate what is happening right now. For example, if we're thinking about a meeting that begins in 15 minutes while eating lunch, we may not savor or enjoy the flavors of our food.

Second, this constant focus on the future leads to increased stress and anxiety. Constantly worrying about the next thing can leave us feeling overwhelmed and unable to find peace in the present. Lastly, continually looking ahead causes us to miss opportunities for gratitude. We overlook moments where we could feel thankful, such as a beautiful sunset or a kind word from a friend, by fixating on what's to come.

Living in the Moment

When we express gratitude for what we have right now, we pay more attention to the present and feel more content. For instance, instead of worrying about the future or dwelling on the past, take a few moments each day to think about things you're grateful for, such as a delicious meal, a supportive friend, or a beautiful sunny day. This habit helps you appreciate the positive aspects of your life and keeps you focused on the present, bringing a sense of peace and happiness.

Gratitude and being present are closely linked, as reflected in Jesus's teachings. Practicing gratitude makes us more mindful of the present moment and more appreciative of what we have. Jesus highlighted the importance of recognizing and being thankful for our daily needs when he said, "Give us today our daily bread" (Matthew 6:11). This verse encourages us to value what we have today instead of worrying about what might happen tomorrow. A practical way to do this is by taking a few moments each day to think about three things you are grateful for.

The Essence of Being Present

Being present, or practicing mindfulness, means fully focusing on each moment. It involves being aware of our thoughts, feelings, and surroundings without getting distracted. Another essential aspect of presence is to observe the situation objectively without adding judgment or cause for concern. This approach helps us experience life more fully and improves our overall well-being. Here are some tips to help you be more present:

- *Focus on the Now:* Gratitude means we think about what we have right now, which helps us stay in the moment. For example, feeling thankful for a warm cup of coffee in the morning helps us enjoy that moment instead of rushing through it.

- *Positive Reinforcement:* Gratitude helps us find joy in the present. By noticing the good things happening now, we see the moment more positively, making it easier to stay engaged. Appreciation can be as simple as acknowledging a sunny day or a kind gesture from a friend.

- *Reduce Anxiety:* Worrying about the future or reminiscing about the past can take us away from the present. Gratitude reduces these worries by turning our attention to what is good right now. For example, instead of stressing about an upcoming deadline, being thankful for the support of a helpful teammate can bring us back to the present.

This mutual reinforcement helps us lead a more fulfilling and contented life filled with joy and peace.

Overcoming the "15-minute Syndrome"

To overcome the "15-Minute Syndrome," try some simple strategies. First, focus on what you're doing right now. How many times have you let your thoughts meander to what you need to do when you finish reading? Whether eating dinner, talking with a friend, or cleaning the house, by fully immersing yourself in the present activity, you'll enjoy it more, even if it's something mundane like washing the dishes.

If worries about the future bother you, set specific times to address your fears so they don't interfere with your daily activities. Remember, Jesus promises rest and peace in your worries. As the Bible says in Matthew 11:28-30, "Come to me, all you who are weary and burdened, and I will give you rest. Take my yoke upon you and learn from me, for I am gentle and humble in heart, and you will find rest for your souls. For my yoke is easy, and my burden is light."

Additionally, make gratitude a daily habit. Each day, take a moment to reflect on what you're thankful for; this will boost your happiness. Practicing gratitude reminds us to trust in God and not worry about the future. Following Jesus's advice helps us find peace in the present and counteract the "15-Minute Syndrome." As Jesus said in Matthew 6:28, "Consider the lilies of the field, how they grow: they neither toil nor spin." This verse encourages us to observe nature and see how it thrives without concern for the future.

Adopting this mindset allows us to enjoy life more fully without constantly being busy or stressed about what's next. The following simple practices can help you stay focused on the present and enjoy life more without worrying too much about what's coming next.

- *Enjoy Your Food:* When you eat, take your time and really taste what's on your plate. Notice the flavors and textures, and enjoy each bite.

- *Listen Carefully:* When someone talks to you, listen closely to what they say. Pay attention to their words and feelings; try not to think about what you'll say next.

- *Take Walks Outside:* Go for short walks outside and notice what's around you. Look at the trees, listen to the birds, and feel the sun on your face.

- ***Breathe Deeply:*** Take a moment to take deep breaths throughout the day. Close your eyes and feel your chest rise and fall with each breath.

- ***Be Thankful:*** Before bed, think about three things you're thankful for from your day. It could be anything, like a tasty snack or a fun conversation. Appreciating these things helps you focus on the good stuff happening right now.

Benefits of Mindfulness and Gratitude

Mindfulness means being aware of our thoughts, feelings, and surroundings without getting distracted. This helps us experience life more fully and feel better overall. Gratitude is about appreciating what we have. It also enables us to focus on the good things in our lives. When we are grateful, we are happier and less stressed.

Both mindfulness and gratitude can improve our mental health, helping us be present and enjoy life more. By practicing mindfulness and gratitude every day, we can lead a more fulfilling and peaceful life. As Jesus said, "Therefore I tell you, do not worry about your life, what you will eat or drink; or about your body, what you will wear. Is not life more than food, and the body more than clothes?" (Matthew 6:25). This verse reminds us to focus on the present moment and trust that our needs will be met.

We can find peace and contentment each day by letting go of worry and embracing mindfulness and gratitude. Here are three simple ways to bring mindfulness into your daily routine.

Starting your day with a simple stretching routine can be a mindful practice. As you stretch, pay attention to how your body feels. Notice the sensation in your muscles and joints. Intentional movement helps you connect with your body and start the day mindfully.

Another way to practice being present is by listening to music. Set aside time to enjoy your favorite songs without distractions. Focus on the instruments, the melody, and the lyrics. Let yourself fully experience the music and notice how it makes you feel.

Creating a gratitude jar is a tangible way to cultivate appreciation. Keep a jar and small pieces of paper in your home. Write down something you're thankful for each day and put it in the jar. At the end of the month, read through all the notes to remind yourself of the positive things in your life.

Living in the moment appreciates the present, finds gratitude in everyday experiences, and trusts God's guidance. Jesus' teachings remind us to let go of worries about the future and find solace in the present. As we embrace each moment with faith and gratitude, we can overcome the "15-Minute Syndrome" and experience greater joy and fulfillment in our lives.

So, let's take a deep breath, focus on the here and now, and find comfort in knowing we are not alone on this journey. With Jesus by our side, we can find rest for our souls and live each moment to the fullest.

And whatever you do, whether in word or deed,
do it all in the name of the Lord Jesus,
giving thanks to God the Father through him.
—Colossians 3:17

CHAPTER 3

CULTIVATING GRATITUDE DAILY

Cultivating daily gratitude means regularly noticing and appreciating the good things in our lives. We recognize the positive aspects and feel thankful for them, no matter how small they seem.

Gratitude practices are simple daily actions that focus on the good things in your life. Gratitude means being thankful for what you have. When you practice gratitude regularly, it can make you feel happier and less stressed.

Exploring gratitude is like discovering a treasure trove with immediate joy and lasting contentment. It's not just a fleeting feeling but a habit we can cultivate every day. By living with gratitude, we find happiness in the little moments and build a habit of appreciating what we have. Try these ideas to practice daily gratitude:

1. *Gratitude Photo Challenge:* Capture moments of gratitude through photography by taking a daily photo of something you're thankful for. It could be a beautiful sunset, a colorful flower blooming in your garden, or a cozy corner of your home. Reviewing these photos at the end of each week can serve as a visual reminder of the abundance in your life.

2. *Gratitude Meditation*: Incorporate a short gratitude meditation into your daily routine. While sitting quietly, focus on your breath and allow feelings of gratitude for the blessings in your life to flow through. You can silently repeat gratitude affirmations or visualize moments of joy and abundance.

3. *Share Gratitude at Mealtimes:* Each family member can share something they are thankful for during dinner. Sharing in this way can strengthen family bonds and create a positive atmosphere.

4. *Express Gratitude Upon Waking:* Start your day by thinking of a few things for which you are grateful. Waking with a grateful attitude sets a positive tone for the rest of the day.

5. *Bedtime Gratitude Practice:* Reflect on your day before sleeping and identify what you appreciated most. This reflection can help you end the day on a positive note and enjoy better sleep.

6. *Soothe Challenges with Gratitude:* When faced with a challenge, before addressing the situation, name three to five things you're grateful for. This practice can put you in a more open and positive mindset before jumping in to solve the problem.

7. *Gratitude Letter:* A gratitude letter is simply a note of thanks you write to someone who has affected your life in a positive way. Michigan State University says writing such a letter is an excellent way to show appreciation for someone who has made a difference to you. It might not seem like a big deal, but brain imaging studies show that writing a gratitude letter creates strong, lasting positive feelings for both the writer and the recipient.[2]

8. *Gratitude Rituals:* Create simple rituals or traditions that celebrate gratitude in your daily routine. A ritual could involve lighting a candle and reflecting on your blessings each morning, saying a prayer of thanks before meals, or ending the day with a gratitude journaling session where you write down three things you're thankful for from the day. Reflecting on Jesus's teaching in John 15:13, "Greater love has no one than this: to lay down one's life for one's friends," reminds us of the profound value of gratitude in our relationships.

Gratitude means more than just recognizing a happy feeling. It involves noticing and valuing the positive aspects around us... Over the past twenty years, research has shown that gratitude benefits many areas of our lives, improving our mental and physical health. The Greater Good Science Center at the University of California, Berkeley, highlights that gratitude acts as "social glue," strengthening our relationships.

---

[2]   Zerbe, Leah. *Dr. Axe.* "How to Write a Gratitude Letter." January 2, 2023. https://draxe.com/health/gratitude-letter/

Robert Emmons, a leading expert on gratitude, explains that gratitude has two parts: recognizing the good around us and acknowledging that this goodness often comes from outside ourselves, such as from other people or nature. This perspective helps us see how much others contribute to our well-being. Gratitude isn't just a fleeting emotion. Studies show that writing gratitude letters or keeping a gratitude journal can significantly boost mental health and life satisfaction, even changing our brains. For example, a study called "The Science of Gratitude," completed by the Greater Good Science Center, found:

> ...[P]articipants who had written gratitude letters in a therapeutic intervention expressed more gratitude and had more activity three months later in their pregenual anterior cingulate cortex, an area involved in predicting the outcomes of actions, suggesting that a simple gratitude intervention can have lasting brain changes even months after the intervention ends.[3]

Practicing gratitude also enhances our ability to recall positive experiences, making it easier to find joy during difficult times. Nancy Davis Kho, author of "The Thank-You Project: Cultivating Happiness One Letter of Gratitude at a Time," found that writing thank-you letters helped her stay positive and resilient. When she embarked on her journey to write fifty thank you letters and complete her book,

---

[3] Allen, Summer, PhD. *Greater Good Science Center.* "The Science of Gratitude" Accessed May 23, 2023. https://ggsc.berkeley.edu/images/uploads/GGSC-JTF_White_Paper-Gratitude-FINAL.pdf

Kho summarizes the project in three simple steps, done repeatedly:

- See the people, places, and things that make your life richer.

- Say something to acknowledge your good fortune in your letters.

- And, by keeping copies of the letters to reread, savor the generosity and support that surrounds you.[4]

An article titled "Is Gratitude Good for Your Health?"[5] by Summer Allen, Ph.D., a Research/Writing Fellow at the Greater Good Science Center (GGSC), discusses whether gratitude leads to better health, if good health makes people more grateful, or if something else affects both gratitude and health. Studies show that grateful people may be healthier, but it's also possible that people in poorer health find it harder to feel grateful. Researchers are now investigating whether activities promoting gratitude improve health.

The GGSC's Thnx4 project found that people who kept an online gratitude journal for two weeks reported an improvement in their physical health. They experienced fewer headaches, less stomach pain, clearer skin, and reduced

---

4   Davis-Kho, Nancy. *Greater Good Magazine.* "What Happened When I Wrote My Mom A Thank-You Letter." November 22, 2019. https://greatergood.berkeley.edu/article/item/ what_happened_when_i_wrote_my_mom_a_thank_you_letter

5   Allen, Summer. *Greater Good Magazine.* "Is gratitude good for your health?" March 5, 2018. https://greatergood.berkeley.edu/article/ item/is_gratitude_good_for_your_health

congestion. These findings align with a 2003 study by Robert Emmons and Michael McCullough. They found that college students who wrote about things they were grateful for once a week for ten weeks had fewer physical symptoms compared to those who wrote about daily events or problems.[6]

Overall, cultivating gratitude offers numerous benefits, from boosting mood and mental health to improving physical well-being and strengthening relationships. By practicing gratitude, we can learn to see the bigger picture, navigate challenges resiliently, and appreciate the goodness in our lives.

Personal Relationship: Family and Friends

Sara Algoe, an assistant professor in the Department of Psychology and Neuroscience at the University of North Carolina at Chapel Hill, developed the "find-remind-and-bind" theory of gratitude.[7] This theory suggests that gratitude is important because it helps us find good people, appreciate our current relationships, and maintain them. When we express thanks, it can motivate us to improve ourselves and strengthen our connections with others. Understanding this can help us see how valuable gratitude is in our friendships and social interactions.

---

[6] Allen, Summer, PhD. *Greater Good Science Center*. "The Science of Gratitude."May 2018.https://ggsc.berkeley.edu/images/uploads/ GGSC-JTF_White_Paper-Gratitude-FINAL.pdf

[7] Sara B. Algoe, "Find, Remind, and Bind: The Functions of Gratitude in Everyday Relationships," *Social and Personality Psychology Compass* 6, no. 6 (May 31, 2012): 455–69, https://doi. org/10.1111/j.1751-9004.2012.00439.x.

Sara Algoe's research also highlights that gratitude acts like a "booster shot," enhancing communication and connection in romantic relationships. Her studies indicate that couples who express gratitude feel more satisfied and connected, reinforcing the positive impact of gratitude on relationships, as outlined in her theory.

Practicing gratitude together as a family or with friends also has the potential to deepen these relationships. For example, one family found that discussing what they're grateful for brought them closer together.[8]

In personal relationships, expressing gratitude fosters a deeper sense of connection and appreciation. We strengthen our bonds when we acknowledge and thank our partners, friends, and family for their kindness, support, and love. It creates a positive feedback loop, where acts of gratitude are reciprocated, leading to a cycle of mutual appreciation and affection. For instance, thanking a family member for a simple gesture, like cooking a meal or offering support during a tough time, reinforces feelings of love and respect, creating a desire to continue serving the family in this way.

Research from "The Science of Gratitude" study mentioned earlier confirms the role gratitude plays in reciprocity with others.

Practicing gratitude may increase brain activity related to predicting how our actions affect other people. "To the extent one predicts and evaluates the likely effects of one's

---

[8]   Algoe, S. B., Gable, S. L., & Maisel, N. C. .*Wiley Online Library.* "It's the little things: Everyday gratitude as a booster shot for romantic relationships." *Personal Relationships,* May 21, 2010. https://doi.org/10.1111/j.1475-6811.2010.01273.x

actions on others," they write, "one might be more willing to direct those actions towards having a positive impact on others."[9]

Professional Relationships: Teammates and Peers

In the workplace, gratitude can greatly enhance team dynamics and job satisfaction. Showing appreciation for teammates' efforts and contributions helps create a supportive and collaborative atmosphere. When colleagues feel valued and recognized, they are more motivated, productive, and engaged in their work. A simple "thank you" or acknowledgment of someone's effort in a team meeting can significantly build a positive and cohesive team culture.

Gratitude can help solve conflicts and encourage forgiveness in relationships. By recognizing and expressing thanks for the good parts of a person or situation, even during disagreements, we can ease tensions and support making peace. It allows us to shift our perspective from grievances to gratitude, fostering empathy and understanding.

Furthermore, practicing gratitude in relationships cultivates a culture of kindness and generosity. When we consistently express gratitude towards our loved ones, we create an environment where acts of kindness and appreciation become the norm, enriching the quality of our interactions and fostering a sense of harmony.

Gratitude plays a transformative role in relationships, enriching them with positivity, connection, and

---

[9]   Allen, Summer, PhD. *Greater Good Science Center.* "The Science of Gratitude. May 2018. https://ggsc.berkeley.edu/images/uploads/GGSC-JTF_White_Paper-Gratitude-FINAL.pdf

understanding. Gratitude is a beacon of light, guiding us to uplift and empower those around us.

Here are some simple ways you can use gratitude to improve your mental health and relationships:

1. *Say Thank You Often:* Make it a habit to say "Thank you" to the people around you for even small things. It shows appreciation and makes everyone feel good. "And whatever you do, whether in word or deed, do it all in the name of the Lord Jesus, giving thanks to God the Father through him" (Colossians 3:17). This verse emphasizes the importance of expressing gratitude in everything we do, attributing our thankfulness to God. It reminds us to incorporate gratitude into our daily interactions and activities to honor Jesus and acknowledge the blessings we receive.

2. *Celebrate Success Together:* When someone achieves something, celebrate with them. It could be finishing a project or even completing something they were nervous about.

3. *Let Go of Grudges:* If someone upsets you, try to forgive them instead of holding onto bad feelings. Letting go of the pain helps you feel better and strengthens your relationships.

4. *Help Each Other:* Offer help and support to your friends and family when they need it. It makes them feel loved and supported.

5. *Do Nice Things:* Complete small acts of kindness, like making someone a cup of tea or sharing a compliment, can make a big difference in how they feel.

6. *Spend Time Together:* Make time to hang out with the people you care about. The activity, whether it's a walk, having a conversation, cooking a meal, or watching a movie, is less important than being present. Spending time together strengthens your bond and makes everyone feel appreciated..

Gratitude Habit Stack

The term "habit stacking" was first introduced by author S. J. Scott in his 2014 book, *Habit Stacking: 97 Small Life Changes That Take Five Minutes or Less.*[10] However, it gained widespread popularity through James Clear's bestselling book, *Atomic Habits.*[11] Habit stacking leverages the routines we already perform automatically. When you attach a new habit to something you already do regularly, you're habit stacking.

Though effective, habit stacking can be challenging. Building good habits isn't foolproof because our brains work differently, and we become less inclined to form new habits as we age.

Habit stacking invites us to develop a new habit by connecting it to something we already do. A type of implementation intention, instead of linking your new habit to a specific time and place, you link it to an existing habit.

In this case, combining gratitude practices with daily activities, like sending thank-you emails or socializing with

---

[10]   S. J. Scott, *Habit Stacking: 97 Small Life Changes That Take Five Minutes or Less* (Lexington, KY: Archangel Ink, 2014).

[11]   1. James Clear, *Atomic Habits: Tiny Changes, Remarkable Results: An Easy & Proven Way to Build Good Habits & Break Bad Ones* (New York, NY: Avery, 2018).

coworkers outside of work hours, helps establish a regular habit of appreciating others and fostering stronger relationships in the workplace. By linking gratitude with these actions, individuals can cultivate a more positive work environment and enhance personal well-being simultaneously.

Here are a few examples of "gratitude habit stacks" that not only encourage gratitude but also help build stronger workplace relationships, creating a positive and supportive environment:

- *Thank You Emails:* You're already checking your email every day. To habit stack in gratitude, choose one or two to reply to. Send emails thanking coworkers or team members who have supported you or improved your workday. Recognize their contributions, whether assisting with a project, giving valuable advice, or boosting morale with their positive attitude. Expressing gratitude this way strengthens bonds and promotes teamwork.

- *Socialize Outside of Work:* You eat lunch and dinner every day. Use these regular events to plan social events or outings with coworkers outside of office hours to deepen friendships and show appreciation for their companionship. If your team attends a conference together, schedule an hour or two of fun to show your appreciation for their hard work. Whether having lunch together, organizing team activities, or attending community events as a group, use this informal time together to foster camaraderie, strengthen relationships, and let them know you are thankful for them.

- *Using the Stairs with Gratitude:* When taking the stairs instead of the elevator, add some extra steps to incorporate gratitude prompts. Reflect on being grateful for having a healthy body that allows you to move effortlessly. A nature walk is also a great example of gratitude and habit stacking. When you go for your daily walk, you can add a moment to consider what you're grateful for. For instance, you might appreciate the fresh air, the trees' beauty, and the birds' sound as you walk. This practice combines the healthy habit of walking with the positive habit of gratitude, making your walk more enjoyable and boosting your mental well-being. These habit stacks combine physical activity with a moment of appreciation, reinforcing a positive mindset throughout the day. Doing this regularly creates a meaningful routine that benefits your body and mind.

Adding gratitude to your daily routines can make you feel better, improve relationships, and create a positive work atmosphere. Small actions, like sending thank-you emails and spending time together outside of work, can help you build a habit of gratitude. This encourages teamwork and friendship among colleagues. These habits spread positivity, making work more enjoyable and friendly for everyone involved.

As we journey through life, it's the little moments of gratitude that leave the biggest marks on our hearts. Imagine a small office where everyone does their best to make it through the day. Challenging work and tight deadlines could cause stress, but the culture of appreciation surrounding them keeps the mood light. By weaving gratitude into our daily routines, we introduce a life filled with joy and connection. As this team has discovered, a little gratitude goes a long way in making work and life more meaningful. So, let's embrace the habit of gratitude and watch how it transforms our world, one thank-you at a time. Now, let's explore how overcoming the desire for more can bring even greater contentment.

Keep your lives free from the love of money
and be content with what you have.
—Hebrews 13:5

CHAPTER 4

OVERCOMING THE DESIRE FOR MORE

B ased on our work with gratitude, we've identified five key steps that help individuals transition from future-focused desire to consciously cultivating gratitude and contentment in the here and now. Those five steps are as follows.

CULTIVATING GRATITUDE AND CONTENTMENT

LET GO OF
COMPARISON

PRACTICE
MINDFULNESS

01 02 03 04 05

PRACTICE
GRATITUDE DAILY

EMBRACE
IMPERFECTION

GIVE BACK

Overcoming the Desire for More

Psychologists refer to the constant pursuit of more as "hedonic adaptation." The term "hedonic" relates to the pleasure or displeasure we get from experiences. Hedonism is the belief that seeking pleasure and avoiding pain are our primary motivations. Psychologists Philip Brickman and Donald Campbell first introduced the concept in their 1971 paper, "Hedonic Relativism and Planning the Good Society."[12] Hedonism has the ability to affect our happiness because when we begin to take things for granted, we look for the next thing that will bring us pleasure. Desire and contentment are naturally connected, like two sides of a coin.

But since we see this principle play out in society so blatantly, how can we overcome? A shift in perspective can transform our lives and help us find true contentment.

There was a time when Amanda constantly compared herself to others, always feeling like she lacked something in her life. The achievements and possessions of others seemed to highlight what she didn't have, making her feel inadequate and unsatisfied. But one day, Amanda shifted her focus from what she didn't have to what she did have. She started keeping a gratitude journal, writing down three things she was thankful for daily.

Over time, Amanda noticed a change in her mindset. She began to appreciate the small joys in life—the warmth

---

12   Brickman and Campbell, "Hedonic relativism and planning the good society." 1971. https://www.semanticscholar. org/paper/Hedonic-relativism-and-planning-the-goo d-society-Brickman-Campbell/705b7748c08 bfdd1808d76a6b10a37842a2482ef

of the sun on her face, the laughter of her loved ones, and the simple pleasures of everyday living. By practicing gratitude regularly, Amanda learned to embrace contentment and find joy in the moment.

A common myth is, "If I achieve this or that, I will be happy or content." This kind of thinking launches us into perpetual unfulfillment. We face new challenges every day as we learn and grow. With every achievement, another lies just out of our reach.

Amanda's gratitude practice shows us that choosing to be content and happy in the journey offers better rewards. Her story teaches us that by focusing on gratitude, we can overcome the desire for more and find true happiness right where we are.

The words "desire," "wish," "want," and "crave" all mean to long for something. Desire means strong feelings about something you want to do or achieve. For example, someone might desire to start a new life. Wish usually means a general or temporary longing, often for something that might be hard to get. When we focus on the things we want but do not yet have, we focus on the absence of or our lack of what we want, which, in turn, reveals more of what's missing in our life.

It's common to always want more money, possessions, and success. But constantly chasing after bigger and better can lead to dissatisfaction and stress. However, there are ways to overcome this desire for more and find contentment with what we already have.

Chase after Gratitude and Contentment

Gratitude and contentment are closely intertwined concepts. You can have all the money and success in the world. But without gratitude, no matter what you achieve, life won't feel any better. Everything good gets lost because we take it for granted. This future-focused mindset is why we often want more in life—more friends, money, and status. But the real question we must ask is, "How can we ever have enough if we don't appreciate what we already have?"

As mentioned above, this hamster wheel of chasing more is called hedonic adaptation, and much of the world is trapped by it. Gratitude is a good way to bypass chasing "more" and be thankful for all the goodness you've accumulated in your life.

Saying thank you is common, but practicing gratitude and regularly focusing on the good parts of life is more than just good manners. It can be a powerful habit for your health.

According to an article by UCLA Health, practicing gratitude for fifteen minutes a day, five days a week, for at least six weeks, can improve your mental wellness and possibly change your outlook on life.[13] Gratitude can also have positive effects on your physical health. The biggest health benefits of gratitude come when it becomes a regular habit and part of one's thinking. However, even setting aside a little time each day or week to focus on gratitude can be helpful.

1. *Help Reduce Depression*: Gratitude can help reduce symptoms of depression. People who practice

---

[13] *UCLA Health.* "Health Benefits of Gratitude." March 22, 2023. https://www.uclahealth.org/news/article/health-benefits-gratitude

gratitude often feel more satisfied with life, have stronger relationships, and higher self-esteem compared to those who don't. Depressed individuals might practice gratitude less frequently, but being grateful can ease depression symptoms, helping individuals see the good things they have.

2. *Reduce Anxiety:* Gratitude has the potential to aid in managing anxiety. Regularly practicing gratitude can fight negative thoughts by focusing on the present. When worried about the past or future, finding something to be grateful for right now can break the cycle of negative thoughts and bring the mind back to the present.

3. *Support Heart Health:* Many benefits of gratitude also contribute to heart health. Reducing symptoms of depression, improving sleep, and maintaining a good diet and exercise routine can lower the risk of heart disease. Studies show that a grateful mindset positively impacts heart health markers. Keeping a gratitude journal can significantly lower diastolic blood pressure, the pressure in the arteries between heartbeats. Even thinking grateful thoughts, without writing them down, can help by slowing and regulating breathing to match the heartbeat.

4. *Enhance Sleep:* Grateful people tend to pursue goals that make them feel good, promoting healthy actions like eating well and exercising regularly, which support better sleep. Practicing gratitude often lessens stress, anxiety, and depression, factors affecting sleep quality and duration.

Stories and Tips for Finding Contentment

In his article "Embracing Change: A Journey Towards Personal Growth and Success," Leo Babauta says,

> In my life, I've learned to be better at the skill of contentment (not that I'm perfect, but I've learned). I am happy with my life. I am happy with myself. I'm happy with where I am professionally and don't seek to add more readers, pageviews, or income. I'm happy wherever I am.
>
> And while many might say, "Sure, you can say that now that you've reached a certain level of success," I think that's wrong. Many people who achieve success don't find contentment, are always driven to want more, and are unhappy with themselves. Many people who are poor or don't have a "successful" career have also found contentment. And what's more, I think finding contentment has driven any success that I've found—it helped me get out of debt, it helped me change my habits, and become a better husband, father, friend, and collaborator, perhaps even a better writer.
>
> Worst of all, with the attitude of "you can be content because you're successful," is that people who say this are dismissing the path of contentment...when it's something they can do right now. Not later, when they reach certain goals or a certain level of financial success.[14]

---

[14] Babauta, Leo. *Zen Habits.* "A Guide to Practical Contentment" Accessed May 23, 2025.. https://zenhabits.net/contentment

The Gap and The Gain Theory

According to author Dan Sullivan, "The way to measure your progress is backward against where you started, not against your ideal." As discussed in Chapter Three, Gap-thinking fixates on the disparity between current reality and future aspirations, while Gain-thinking highlights the strides already achieved. [15] Embracing these perspectives fosters gratitude for progress and cultivates a mindset geared toward continuous improvement and fulfillment.

When we compare ourselves to our ideal, we always fall in "the GAP." But when we compare ourselves to how we used to be, we see how far we've progressed in "the GAIN."

Dan Sullivan, founder of Strategic Coach, and Dr. Benjamin Hardy's book, *The Gap and the Gain,* introduce a transformative concept that helps us navigate our journey toward personal and professional goals. The Gap and the Gain concept encourages us to view our progress from two perspectives: focusing not just on the distance between our current state and our ideal goals (the gap) but also celebrating the strides we've made from our starting point (the gain). And while the concept applies to many areas of life, its implications for how we approach our finances and goal-setting are profound. This infographic perfectly illustrates the concept: [16]

---

[15]   Dan Sullivan and Benjamin Hardy.
[16]   Maurer, Tim. *Forbes.* "Are You Stuck in the Gap or Living in the Gain?" January 28, 2024. https://www.forbes.com/sites/timmaurer/2024/01/28/are-you-stuck-in-the-gap-or-living-in-the-gain/

THE GAP AND THE GAIN

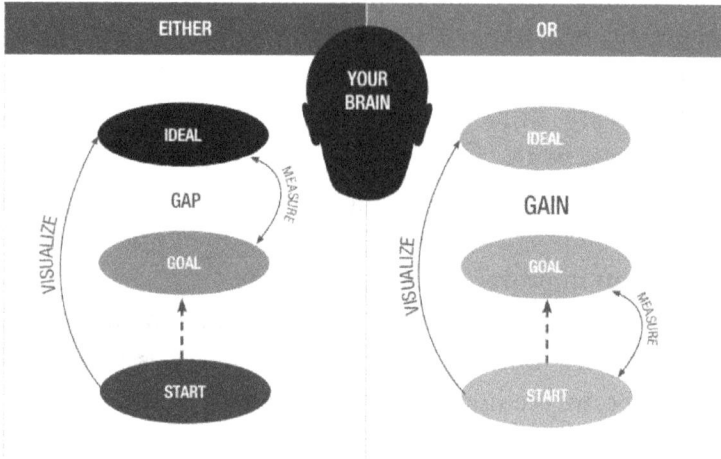

Embracing this dual approach allows us to cultivate a healthier and more balanced outlook on our achievements, fostering appreciation for our continuous growth.

Finding Faith Beyond Money

A healthy relationship with money can lead to a life filled with good deeds and positive outcomes. People often feel safe and secure when they have money in the bank. At times, having plenty of money makes one feel on top of the world. The problem arises when money and God enter the same conversation. The more money one has, the more blessed they feel. More money means more of God in life. At least, that's what many think.

With that mindset, faith can take a big hit when money starts to run out. It is tough to understand why money comes in and leaves so quickly. God left? Did He decide not to help? Did I do something wrong? Has He moved on to others?

As the Bible says in Hebrews 13:5, "Keep your lives free from the love of money and be content with what you have because God has said, 'Never will I leave you; never will I forsake you.'"

We must remember that security and blessings don't come from money alone. While financial stability can bring temporary comfort, equating wealth with divine favor can lead to disappointment and spiritual emptiness when financial circumstances change. Instead of relying solely on material wealth, finding contentment in what we have and trusting in a deeper spiritual connection brings lasting peace. As Hebrews 13 reminds us, God promises to never abandon us, offering a steadfast presence that transcends earthly riches.

Fulfillment and Big Dreams

Gratitude can help people love what they're doing and appreciate where they are now, but it also helps them aim for more. Here are five ways to use gratitude to boost the pursuit of dreams.

- *Appreciate Where You Are Right Now:* Start by being grateful for where you are, even if you're far from your dreams. As Melody Beattie, an American author of self-help books on codependent relationships, said, "Gratitude turns what we have into enough and more." This makes it easier to be happy with your current situation. There's always something to be grateful for. For example, if the dream is to run a Mexican food truck, be thankful for the vision, cooking skills, and the job that supports that dream.

- *Propel Yourself into Action:* Gratitude can motivate action toward dreams. When action is needed, ask why it will be something to be grateful for. Use this reason as motivation. This can help with simple tasks like completing a passport application or facing fears like starting a blog.

- *Stay Motivated:* Achieving a dream takes time. Use gratitude to stay motivated by acknowledging and appreciating the small steps toward the dream. Celebrate mini-milestones, like getting a first client or booking a flight.

- *Appreciate Your Dream as if It's Already Achieved:* Be grateful for the dream as if it's already a reality. Imagine how it will feel when the dream comes true, and identify why it will be something to be grateful for. For example, if you dream of owning a successful bakery, practice being thankful for creating delicious treats, happy customers, and the joy of running your own business.

In embracing gratitude, individuals find personal fulfillment and a pathway to greater aspirations. By appreciating the present and fostering gratitude for each step toward their dreams, they learn to find contentment while striving for more. Gratitude fuels actions, motivates through challenges, and keeps focus on the joy of pursuing passions. Whether celebrating small victories or envisioning dreams as realities, harnessing the power of gratitude enriches journeys and inspires others to do the same.

Give thanks in all circumstances;
for this is God's will for you in Christ Jesus.
—1 Thessalonians 5:18

CHAPTER 5

PROGRESSING IN GRATITUDE

There are only two ways to live your life. One is as though nothing is a miracle. The other is as though everything is a miracle.
—Albert Einstein

Maya was leading a team at work when they were introduced to a new software system that felt overwhelming. She couldn't figure it out, making her feel like she was failing—not just at the software, but as a leader. Pressure built quickly. In her frustration, she began lashing out at her team with sarcastic comments like, "This should be easy for you." But underneath it all, she didn't feel capable.

Her team picked up on the tension. Morale dropped. Motivation disappeared. The atmosphere shifted from collaborative to cautious, and nobody was thriving.

After speaking with a mentor, Maya realized something needed to change. She restructured her approach, offering resources, cutting unnecessary meetings, and carving out daily time for training and growth. Mornings became team learning time. Afternoons focused on problem-solving and exploration. In the evenings, they paused to reflect and celebrate the day's small wins.

What followed wasn't just technical progress—it was a cultural shift. In just two weeks, the team not only understood the software, they became energized by the process. Gratitude had crept in and reshaped everything. The team started thanking Maya for her leadership and encouraging one another for small breakthroughs. Momentum was no longer built on pressure but on progress.

What is Progress?

Progress isn't always big or flashy. It's not always a leap forward or a major accomplishment. Most of the time, progress looks like small, intentional steps in the right direction. It's the steady effort to grow, even when the results aren't immediate.

Progress can show up as personal development, professional wins, or positive shifts in mindset. Sometimes it feels like you're gaining ground fast. Other times, it feels like you're crawling—one step forward, three steps back. But either way, you're moving. You're trying. And that matters.

True progress isn't measured by perfection—it's measured by movement.

Understanding Failure and Progress

Failure is success in progress.
—Albert Einstein

This quote reframes how we think about failure. Instead of seeing failure as the opposite of success, Einstein saw it as a necessary part of progress.

Failure and progress go hand in hand. You can't grow without friction. You can't improve without feedback. And often, that feedback comes through failure.

The difference-maker is how we respond. Failure can shut us down—or it can refine us. When we're willing to look at failure as a teacher rather than a label, we stay in motion. And motion, even when messy, is a sign of life.

What is Failure?

Deborah Moggach, an English novelist and screenwriter, once said, "The only real failure is the failure to try, and the measure of success is how we cope with disappointment." Failure isn't something to be ashamed of or afraid of. It's not a weakness. It's a signal. It shows us what needs attention and invites us to come back stronger. In fact, failure can offer some of life's greatest advantages. It has the power to push us to grow, fight harder, and sharpen our focus on what truly matters.

Here are just a few ways failure can shape us for the better:

Failure Opens New Doors

Every time we fall short, we're given a chance to look at things differently. Failure teaches us what didn't work and gives us space to try again with more clarity and creativity. When we lean into those lessons, we're more likely to discover fresh solutions and strategies that move us closer to success. Seeing failure as a learning opportunity keeps us flexible, innovative, and forward-focused.

Failure Makes Us Real

Failure humbles us. It strips away our ego and reminds us we're human. And in that humility, we find something powerful: authenticity. When we own our struggles and stop pretending to have it all together, we earn trust—from others and from ourselves. We show we're not afraid of the journey, we're not afraid to grow, and we're not giving up just because it's hard.

Failure Builds Resilience

Facing setbacks gives us grit. It trains us to stand back up, even when it would be easier to quit. Every failure builds mental and emotional strength—if we allow it. It shapes how we respond to stress, how we adapt, and how we persevere when circumstances get tough. With each failure we overcome, we gain the confidence to face the next one with greater determination.

Failure Creates Perseverance

You don't get perseverance from winning—you get it from pushing through when things fall apart. Failure teaches us to keep moving even when progress is slow, the path is unclear, or the outcome feels uncertain. And in that persistence, we develop staying power. We learn how to hold onto our vision, even when everything in us wants to give up.

Here's the truth: failure can benefit anyone. We all grow from it. And some of the world's most powerful success stories were shaped by it, including Steve Jobs.

Steve Jobs, the legendary entrepreneur and co-founder of Apple, built his legacy through a journey marked by bold risks and big setbacks. He launched Apple in 1976 from his parents' garage, creating the Apple I and the wildly successful Apple II. His partnership with Steve Wozniak was game-changing—together, they simplified hardware designs and shaped early personal computing.

But it wasn't all wins. In 1985, the board forced Jobs out of the very company he helped create. Most would've crumbled under the weight of that disappointment. But Jobs didn't stop. He launched NeXT, and later acquired Pixar—ventures that stretched him as a leader and taught him the value of patience, vision, and collaboration.

When Jobs returned to Apple in 1997, he came back stronger. He trimmed down the bloated product line, centered the company on innovation, and introduced game-changing ideas like the iMac, iPod, iPhone, and iPad. These weren't just products—they were cultural shifts. And they cemented his place as one of the most impactful visionaries of our time.

What made Jobs legendary wasn't perfection. It was his ability to rebound. He refused to let failure be the final word. Every setback sharpened his purpose and refined his leadership. The years he spent away from Apple weren't wasted—they allowed him to become the leader Apple needed.

His story is a powerful reminder: failure doesn't mean the end. It might actually be the beginning of something greater. Jobs' journey continues to inspire entrepreneurs, creators, and dreamers across the world. Because through it all—every rejection, every challenge, every misstep—he never stopped learning, growing, and pushing forward.

What is Perfection?

Perfection is the idea of getting something exactly right—flawless, error-free, and completely dialed in. It means hitting an ideal standard where there are no mistakes, everything lines up, and the result matches the vision exactly. And while that kind of precision is admirable, it often comes with a cost—time, energy, and resources. In some areas, it's absolutely worth it. In fact, it's necessary.

Think about it: an annual report to the board, syncing a soundtrack to a video, delivering a keynote speech—those moments demand excellence. They're high-stakes and high-visibility, and the details matter. In business, certain financial metrics are the same. Growing your Net Operating Income year after year, meeting investment benchmarks, submitting accounting reports, and filing taxes—these are places where getting it right isn't optional. It's essential.

However, not everything in life or leadership needs to be perfect. There are plenty of times when *getting it done is better than getting it perfect.* Updating your team on progress, submitting a weekly report, cleaning the house—these don't require flawless execution. They require movement. Action. Follow-through.

Knowing the difference is a mark of wisdom. Aim for perfection when it counts. But don't let it slow you down where it doesn't.

Prioritizing Progress Over Perfection

Continual progress pushes us to keep learning and growing by helping us view mistakes as stepping stones instead of stop signs. When perfection is the goal, we often get trapped in the fear of messing up, which prevents us from trying something new. Perfectionism expects instant results without error, but real growth happens through experimentation. Choosing progress over perfection frees us up to fail, learn, and try again. It sparks creativity and invites new ideas, while perfectionism tends to shut both down out of fear of being wrong or judged.

There's also a major mental health benefit to focusing on progress. The pursuit of perfection brings constant pressure—pressure to perform, to get everything exactly right, to avoid failure at all costs. That weight often leads to anxiety, burnout, and the belief that we're never enough. But when we allow ourselves to learn through mistakes, we create space for compassion. We lower the pressure, stay grounded, and live with more balance. Celebrating small wins builds momentum, boosts our mood, and improves our overall well-being, no matter how small the steps.

As humans, we often idolize perfection. We believe the goal is to be flawless in every area. And while that might sound noble, it can actually slow us down. Trying to be perfect in everything often stunts creativity, discourages risk-taking, and limits growth. Progress, on the other hand, is realistic and achievable. It works with time, budget, and capacity—and it keeps us moving forward. For personal and professional development, this mindset shift is key. Instead of chasing an unreachable standard, we start to value what we're learning, how we're evolving, and who we're becoming.

Let's unpack the importance of *Progress > Perfection* in more detail.

Progress > Perfection Lets Us Embrace Trial and Error

When we focus on progress, we view mistakes as part of the journey, not as failures. We stop getting stuck when things go wrong and start asking, "What can this teach me?" This mindset makes room for trial and error, which is essential for developing wisdom. We experiment, adjust, and try again. That rhythm creates flexibility, resilience, and a willingness to keep going even when results aren't instant.

Progress > Perfection Encourages New Ideas

Trying to be perfect kills creativity. The pressure to avoid mistakes or criticism holds us back from thinking differently. That fear of failure—what some call "creativity paralysis"—stifles innovation. But a progress-driven mindset gives us the freedom to explore. The first version might not be great, but that's okay. Trying again, making adjustments, and thinking outside the box is how great ideas are born. Some of the best innovations came from messy first attempts that evolved over time.

Progress > Perfection Promotes Mental Well-Being

Perfectionism is exhausting. It creates a nonstop internal loop that says "not good enough," no matter what we achieve. That mindset leads to stress, anxiety, and feeling like a failure even in success. But when we embrace progress, we replace pressure with perspective. We see each setback as a lesson, not a personal flaw. That shift gives us more realistic expectations, healthier goals, and a deeper sense of peace as we move through both wins and challenges.

The Bottom Line

If you wait until everything is perfect before taking action, you'll stay stuck. The pursuit of 100 percent completion can keep you frozen in the gap between where you are and where you want to be. Set your sights on movement, not mastery. Even if you're only at 80 percent, move forward. Keep going.

Chasing Ideas that Change the World

James Dyson's path to entrepreneurial success is one defined by grit, vision, and a mindset that sees failure as a gift. His breakthrough in vacuum technology wasn't an overnight success—it came after years of trial and error. Over the course of four relentless years, he developed 5,127 prototypes before finally creating the G-Force: a bagless cyclonic vacuum cleaner that changed the industry. At first, British retailers didn't want it. They weren't ready to abandon vacuum bags. But Dyson believed in what he built. And when the G-Force launched in Japan in 1986, it took off, eventually achieving global recognition and transforming the cleaning industry.

Not every product was a win. The CR01 washing machine, for example, was discontinued. But setbacks like that didn't derail him. Dyson's focus never wavered. He kept solving problems. Kept innovating. And through it all, he leaned into the belief that failure isn't something to fear—it's something to learn from. His journey is a masterclass in persistence.

For entrepreneurs, Dyson's story offers powerful take-aways. His resilience is undeniable. He didn't back down in the face of rejection. Instead, he saw each obstacle as something to learn from. His obsession with solving real-world problems led him to push boundaries again and again. Rather than fearing failure, he used it as fuel—revising, testing, and refining until the results matched the vision. He didn't limit his focus to one market; he thought globally from day one. He didn't want to make just another product. He wanted to create something that would matter everywhere.

His approach to design was never static. Dyson believed in constant iteration—improving, adjusting, testing again. That discipline created a culture of excellence in his company and helped him stay at the forefront of innovation. Through every win and every misstep, his mindset remained the same: improve, adapt, grow.

But Dyson's legacy isn't just about innovation—it's about gratitude. His ability to stick with his vision, learn from failure, and stay focused on long-term impact speaks to a deeper awareness. He knew the tough moments—the rejections, the prototypes that didn't work, the products that didn't take off—were part of the process, and he was thankful for all of it.

James Dyson's story reminds us that success doesn't come from avoiding failure. It comes from welcoming it, learning from it, and letting it sharpen your mission. His bold thinking, resilient spirit, and global mindset continue to inspire a new generation of entrepreneurs and remind us that every challenge on the road to success is an opportunity to grow.

Gratitude Challenge for Entrepreneurs

As you've seen through the journeys of Steve Jobs and James Dyson, entrepreneurs are wired differently. They're driven by a unique kind of vision—one fueled by hope, purpose, and the desire to bring something new into the world. Often, that vision is misunderstood. It's unseen, questioned, even mocked by others. Most people don't get it. Just think about Thomas Edison and his 10,000 attempts to invent the light bulb. Can you imagine how many people quietly walked away after attempt number 100? Even the most supportive likely started to doubt. That's how it goes for most—when something doesn't work quickly, they give up.

But that's not the way entrepreneurs operate—especially those walking in step with God's purpose. When things get hard, they don't just rely on grit—they anchor to truth. Galatians 6:9 becomes their guide:

"Let us not become weary in doing good, for at the proper time we will reap a harvest if we do not give up."

That's the difference. **Entrepreneurs don't quit.** They don't abandon the vision. They understand it was planted in them by something greater. They know the calling they carry has divine backing, and this drives them to persevere—not just for their own success, but for the good of others, for the good of the world.

Because the vision pulls them forward, entrepreneurs keep stretching boundaries. They don't settle. The world may have been content with flip phones, but Steve Jobs took it further and introduced the iPhone. It wasn't about satisfying what existed; it was about reimagining what could be. His persistence and willingness to keep innovating unlocked a new era of communication. And those limits? They'll be pushed again by the next generation of bold thinkers who refuse to stop.

But there's a tension that comes with this kind of drive. The very thing that fuels entrepreneurs—this sense of divine discontentment—also makes contentment so elusive. When you're constantly reaching toward a greater vision, it's hard to sit still in the moment. You see what's missing. You feel what's not yet finished. And when you reach the goal, the vision expands. There's always another level.

For the driven entrepreneur, contentment can feel more like a quick pit stop in a high-speed race than a moment of resting in the victory. That's why disciplines like gratitude, celebrating progress, focusing on the gain instead of the gap, and staying spiritually grounded are not optional;

they're essential. They reconnect you to joy and help you stay present. They remind you why the journey matters.

From Steve Jobs' bounce-back moments to Maya's leadership breakthrough, we see the power of perspective. We recognize setbacks as catalysts for growth when paired with resilience and faith. James Dyson's relentless innovation shows that failure isn't the enemy—it's part of the formula for lasting impact.

By leading with gratitude and committing to steady progress, we not only overcome challenges, we grow through them. We build stronger relationships and create meaningful success. And most importantly, we align our hearts with the truth that God calls us to a deeper kind of happiness— not one rooted in external achievement, but in a soul-level appreciation for the journey.

He invites us to choose joy. To learn as we go. We find joy most readily when we give thanks for each step, whether it feels like a breakthrough or a lesson. And in doing so, we discover that the greatest success isn't just in what we accomplish, but in who we become along the way.

ABOUT THE AUTHORS

JEFF HUSTON

As the chief visionary of 3D Money, a private investment group, Jeff Huston understands the complex world of growing and protecting wealth.

For forty years, Jeff has owned and developed businesses. His Unique Ability® of achieving growth-oriented excellence pushes him toward the continual development and progression of leaders and influencers, elevating them to become the best version of themselves. He leads with authenticity and transparency and loves engaging with people who reciprocate.

Jeff co-authored the Amazon best-selling book *Purpose, Passion, and Profit*. He has won several National Achievement awards, been a featured guest on many podcasts, and presented at numerous national conventions.

A Minnesota native, Jeff resides in a small countryside community with his wife, Carol. Together they have two daughters and eight grandchildren.

Connect with Jeff at 3Dmoney.com

A FAITH-BASED ALTERNATIVE INVESTMENT COMPANY

3D Money

3D Money is a real estate investment company dedicated to searching out value-add, cash-flow opportunities in real property.

3DMoney.com

GABE OLSON

An accomplished entrepreneur and leader, Gabe Olson serves as a visionary over multiple companies, including manufacturing, real estate, and agriculture. His work includes an extensive background of over fifteen years in the real estate business, project and property management, and construction.

This Minnesota native and dedicated family man has been happily married to his wife, Andrea, for 18 years. Together, they have three daughters, and Gave finds extreme joy in being a great dad.

Gabe and Andrea co-authored a series of Amazon bestsellers teaching kids about prayer and how to look for God's miracles in everyday life. This is the heart of his work, and he is fueled every day by a deep sense of gratitude for what Christ has done.

Explore the series at TheBigGodBooks.com.

CONNECT WITH GABE

Follow him on Instagram today.

@gabeolsonofficial

A FAITH-BASED ALTERNATIVE INVESTMENT COMPANY

3D Money

3D Money is a real estate investment company dedicated to searching out value-add, cash-flow opportunities in real property.

3DMoney.com